Table of  Content

Life

I write about a lot, but not much about me.
But is that something you are ready to see?
You can guess what is on my mind and that is
a start.
But can you feel what is going on in my heart.
It is not about money or even sex, and to be
honest it is not really that complex.
But for Understanding you would really have
to know JOE.
So please be gentle and take it slow.

Kryptonite

I don't understand at times what is on my
mind.
It seems like at times I am just one step behind.
Do any of us know what it is that we truly
want?
Or should I just put my focus back on blowing
that blunt.
Is attention just too much to ask?
Lol, Look at you now just hiding behind that
mask.
I now know it is has always been for the best.
No since in settling for a C+, on the final test.
My words now have my biggest concern.
Cus over time it has been a lot I have had to
learn.
It is now time that I let my words take flight.
And stop focusing on the Queens who have
that Kryptonite.
©Joseph FbPoet Wilder2013

Got it Bad

We all think that we have it bad.

Like we are the only one who at times get sad.

You never know what hand that you may be given.

All you can do is stay positive and keep on living.

If I could, I wish that I could save us all.

Every Ry Body Yes Every Ry D@mn body would never fall.

I have faith that one day I will get my wish.

And no one ever again we will have to miss.

I know some really choose not to care.

But you can't then turn around and say that life isn't fair.

Every Ry Thang yes every ry thang in this world does not revolve around just you.

So it will take a combined effort of us all if we want to make it thru.

©Joseph FbPoet Wilder2013

Do You

This world is crazy; I just thought that you should know

I am not the smartest, but I am never slow

With life you have to learn how to decipher the bull

Cus it will always be those that try to pull that wool

Like with politics it is funny how when we had Clinton they were banging in Lil Rock

Now we get Obama, and you see shorties murdered in the Chi on eVeRy block

With relationships people are no longer serious they just pass the time

EveRyRybody trying to figure out what is going on in someone else's mind

With religion it is so much we are right, and you are wrong

EveRyRybody want to feel like they are the only ones who belong

But I cannot, and don't want to control what it is that you are trying to do

As long as it doesn't in ANY way negatively affect me, continue to do you

©Joseph FbPoet Wilder2013

Fantasy

When guys are born, we are raised in a GI Joe, HeMan, Spider Man mind frame

Queens are brought up in the Barbie aspect, where she is the independent sexy dame

She has her own job, car, and the raw tip

Then Ken slid thru, and took her convertible whip

They had the baker sets, the ovens preparing you for your next stage in life

N you looked, at Betty, Wilma, and Marge to prepare you to be a good wife

A battle, a war is something that we always did face

With wonder woman, super girl, cat woman, and shera on the side to give us a lil taste

But without the one, you could never have the other

Always another action figure, so you wanna make sure that you don't smother

Guess this is why most queens get older, and want to fight

And guys, we start to base things not on facts, but only on sight

Both sides, are constantly battling trying to figure where they are supposed to be

Bad part about it is deciphering which part is real, and what is just your Fantasy

©Joseph FbPoet Wilder2013

Started at the Bottom now We Here

When I talk about my heritage, I refer to an unwavering strength

Fuc% Prince William, and Kate, we come from the True King, and Queen descent

Now we have no idea what the bottom, or the top is

All we do now is just twerk, and have some kids

I can ask you where your family originated, and most will give me an answer that is real dumb

I know that because of slavery most don't know where it is that they come from

It has nothing to do with this continent, or the Good U.S.

We were brought here by people that just said, Im Sorry We Confess

Read this Book, because yours is wrong

Be like us, if you want to belong

All that we see now in this world, can do a lot more than bring a tear

Because we were already at the Top, now look at us We Are Here!

©Joseph FbPoet Wilder2013

Last Cry

The battle that I have comes from within

It goes beyond family, foe, or friend

I have asked to be directed so that I could see

But what if your teacher is your biggest enemy

So many races, religions, each wanting to pass the blame

Then my question becomes are we really the same

We say that your blood is red just like mine

But we have some that are ready to kill for that dime

I have tried to understand motivations for things people
do

Why is it so hard for others to stay true

When it boils down you don't have the answer, and
neither do I

But a brotha is getting tired of saying that this is My Last
Cry!

©Joseph FbPoet Wilder2013

Power of the P.U.S.S.Y

From the time you hit puberty, for a man it is not the same

Doesn't matter where you are from I know where to place the blame

It will make you fall in love buy that ring, and give a surprise

Or it can turn around, and fool you then victimize

In this world it can bring, or take much power

That means it can bring much love, or eat you up and devour

Make you buy the raw whip, spending those stacks

Then it can have you feenin like you are on crack

The three things brothas luv money, coochie, and drugs

That goes from the softest, down to the street thugs

It will have you babysitting so that it never leaves your eye

N it all stems from the Power Of The P.U.$.$.Y.

©Joseph FbPoetWilder2013

My Story

Humble beginnings were my start

Always tried to keep fantasy, and reality apart

Come on, and take a ride with me so we can raise the bar

Cus if you ride with them, you are never going too far

This is my life, never a game

I need a co-pilot so we can share the fame

Never trying to switch up, and hit your friend

World already F-Up, don't need no more sin

My talents are bipolar, this you can see

For that I have no shame in entering a guilty plea

They ask me, why you chase all of these skirts

That's just a part of coming up in that ChiTown dirt

Not trying to disappear on you, like hokas pokas

Can finally say that a brotha is a lot more focused

Just had to take the time to find out what is the true glory

N I am sticking to it, because this is My Story

©Joseph FbPoet Wilder2013

Change Gone Come

I was born by the lake in Michael Reese hospital

N like the lake I've been staying below underneath it all

Afraid to die but living so hard

Always making sure, that i always play the right card

It has been times, that I didn't think that I would last for
long

Surrounded by people, just trying to belong

It's been times when I have been knocked down on my
knees

N I go to my people, and kindly ask them please

Truth, assistance is all that I ask

But most focus is to just get downtown, and make some
cash

Don't know where I am headed, but I will always
remember where I come from

But I still have faith that a positive change is Going To
Come!

©Joseph FbPoet Wilder 2013

Come N Talk 2 Me

Some people are meant to be Drs., and some are meant to be lawyers

You have your career seekers, and your job employers

The parents whose job is to raise and care for their child

N those without, who can act a lil more wild

People in this world, whose focus is just on a buck

Or the hot ones that just want to f()ck

The kings and queens that are meant to be wed

N those who aren't going to allow, another into their bed

Regardless I can guarantee, that you will never find another like me

So if you want to find out, how about you just Come N Talk 2 Me

©Joseph FbPoet Wilder2013

Surrender to You

There is a story in my life

When you need AnyBody the Most, they are never around.

But they can all pop out the woodworks, when you hit the ground!

After all of the knowledge in life, that I have sowed,

My True Pain, can never ever be told.

The World is so messed up, and the game is so foul.

N that goes all the way back, to the First Mother N Child!

A Story of Pain, is in Each one of our lives.

But So Many are Hypocrites, and want to act surprised!

That is why you gotta keep it 100, and keep your circle tight.

Cus it is a Cold, Cold, Cold World, Not just at night!

See KARMA, is a MF, that act like a BITCH!

Don't have to be a Female, can be your Boy, down to a Snitch!

Times are so different now, and it is NoMore Loyalty.

Now it is Dollar Bills, that EveRyRyBody wanna See!

One of the main reasons, that it is hard for me to trust.

Always trying to figure out, What is True Love, or just Lust?

You Learn in Life, eveRyRybody that smile in your face,
Aint your Friend.

When pain gets unbearable, Most wont be there till thE
End!

Time, will let you know who your True Friends are.

Cus your True Friends, not about to let you slip
underneath that bar!

We Learn though, that things don't always go the way we
plan

N that the Ones who can cut you most, are closest friends
to your Fam!

See it is not about racisim, or even politics.

Like I said Before, we All know those hypocrites!

That always want to front, and just smile in your face.

Then you find out, you done caught a case!

But we ALL need to FIRST step back, N Correct ALL of the
harm that We do.

Cus Until then, I will NEVER be able to EVER,, SURRENDER
TO ANY OF YOU!!!!!!!

Troubled Man

Growing up in life there are things that you learn

Most important, is to focus on things that should have your concern

It will be pluses, but the minuses will try to tear you apart

It will be times that you have to pick yourself up, and have to restart

You learn how to keep things together, and to keep it real

Cus people will bother you, and not care how you feel

People will always try you, one thing that I know for sure

But thru the trials, and tribulations you must endure

We are taught to be fair, and to play by the rules

However they themselves can appear real cruel

Taxes, death, and trouble will always be there

Some of those things in life that just aint fair

Whether uptown or downtown or moving down the line

It will always seem easier if you just cause a crime

No matter where you are, that is something that we all understand

But I refuse to go thru the heartache, and pain of being a Troubled
Man!!!

©Joseph FbPoet Wilder2014

Coming Back Home

It took me some time to finally come around

Never fully appreciated what I had already found

Thought I had it figured out, and my pride got in the way

All my mistakes, in time I will have to pay

Time......Something that we should never waist

I want the full meal, no need for a taste

Had to grow, and understand what it is all about

But not being focused, queens would take me another route

A total bliss, that goes beyond just having fun

For you am the one I want, before all is said n done

To hold you in my arms, and feel all of heavens grace

As I gaze into your eyes n kiss your Pretty Face

A love that I crave, that goes beyond just talking on the phone

So imma need you to get ready,, cus Im Coming Back Home!!!

©Joseph FbPoet Wilder2014

Back N the Day

Am I my brothas keeper? It is a simple Yes, or No!

Too bad most of these brothas only care bout a hoe!

One of the main reasons I always loved my frat!

Our community service goes beyond just wearing a cap.

Of course you can never forget the fam.

But what about the ones that don't really give a d@mn.

At a time, people knew if something happened to them, at least the community still had each other's back!

N that went beyond just making a stack.

When Queens actually knew how to go in the kitchen, N COOK!

N communication was with your mouth, wasn't a FaceBook !

He may have been a rolling stone, but at least he was around.

Now most of these fathers are not in a position to make a sound.

I wish that my people would look at each other, and just feel proud!

N that we ALL are chosen to go beyond the clouds.

But when it comes to my people, why does it have to be a wish?

That part of the past, Trust I Do Miss.

They had faith, and believed that things would be better.

Now they are just focused on making her stay wetter.

Let me stop now, before I say something that I don't wanna say.

But I still believe that we can have the love for each other, that we used to have, Back in the Day!!!

Second Chance

Some may say that I have changed, and for that I take the blame

For my spoken word, can cause lots of pain

I ask that you listen, and you can feel my melody

N I promise that I will always be more, than just a memory

Let My Word shield you, as it continues to ring

So that as you face your inner fears, you will be able to sing

It will be no worries, for I am here to stay

Let my love save you, each and eveRyRyday

But we all know that what should be, and what is, is not the same

At times we have to cleanse ourselves, by walking thru the rain

You can't believe all that you hear or see

You need to feel the warmth of love surrounding you, and me

So tonight as I say my prayers, and start to lie down

I say goodbye to broken promises, and lay them on the ground

For I know, all that we share is a true romance

N I am just blessed to say, that I have been given a Second Chance!!!

©Joseph FbPoet Wilder2014

When it Hurts

You say its Not The Time.

I cant make u see that by just writing a rhyme.

A good friend explained to me that I have to let go of my pain.

If I hold on to my past it will drive me insane.

By holding on to the negative in my past it will block my blessing. And maybe that's why I have never had my wedding.

We all have our good and our bad.

But u cant lose focus over what u may have had.

Im always so focused on helping others smile.

While I block my pain and live in denial.

When it hurts we try to hide it and make it so hard to say.

So I forget/forgive and know that it is now no longer time to play.

Love em All

At a point in life where my heart beats but I no longer feel.

Now I have to always decipher the fake from the real.

Surrounded by so many, always just holding out their hand.

But my true motivation, most will never understand.

Most always want to just make things too complex.

It is a lot more important things, than just having sex.

Some think I do too much, others think I move too fast.

But ya boy is Going to WIN, aint no coming in last!!

I am never trying to confuse, or break anyone's heart.

But my graphics is how I reboot, and hit restart.

If anyone has a problem, you can always just walk away.

It will always be another, before the end of the day.

I try to always stay civil, and put forth my best.

However I've noticed that most want me to fail this test.

Always those that want to compare me with another.

But remember I am an intelligent, yet semi sexy special brother.

With myself I am settled, and don't want to play around.

With, or without, I am already shutting it down.

So I will let you decide, and make that final call.

But I am going to continue to do JOE, and just Luv em All!

©Joseph FbPoet Wilder2015

Divine Glory

These Words are to All, but my grandfather comes to mind.

Joseph Wilder Sr. was always one of a kind.

I raise my hands to the heavens, so his blessings I can receive.

Knowing that he already knew, all we could achieve.

He dealt with the dark roads, and was always a hero to us.

Around the same time that Rosa Parks took a seat on the bus.

He wanted the sins of the past, to become our blessing.

But he knew he had to fight on, and keep on pressing.

He marched to a rhythm, but it was a whole other beat.

To achieve this victory, he did not want to cheat.

Like Dr. King, he knew that we could reach the mountain top.

N that his chilling's, would oneday not have to field the crop.

Without much education, he still had so much wisdom.

Why he never looked back, when it came to our freedom.

He was always told to stand down, but continued to stand up.

Just so that we could always, have a full cup.

He wanted Justice for all, regardless of the color of our skin.

N for us he never gave up, he knew he had to win.

To me, he has always deserved his crown.

Even after physically, he was no longer around

I was young at the time, but was able to at least get seven years

However I still wake up at night, shedding those lonely tears

Over time we have achieved so much, but so much has been lost

But I guess for Divine Glory, will always come with a cost!!!!

©Joseph FbPoet Wilder2015

For the Luv of Money

TCF (The Colored Folks) for hundreds of years have always been used

If you Pan America they have all been abused

From the time we crossed the Atlantic, nothing about their plan has been noble

Now it goes across the Pacific, and now is Global

From the Seaway to the MidLand, down to the Gold Coast

Now it goes International, because the Green means the most

When the slaves would escape, to find Freedom and Liberty

The catchers would lay Chase, from Sea to Sea

As time passed, African Americans were only considered a Fifth Third

Only 3 of us, to 5 of them were observed by the Federal Reserve

Then came the Civil Rights movement, and we were able to move to the big Citi

We could now cross the Parkway, and think that we could be fancy

But like that Novus Ordo Seclorum, that Annuit Coeptis will always be there

Its just sad to me, that most of My People really don't care!!!!!

©Joseph FbPoet Wilder2015

Love

My heart has reached out many times before,

but my mind was never ready for what was in store. I
carried on unaware day to day,

never thinking true love could come my way.

But for me I had to learn the meaning of true love.

And how to respect my gifts from the man above.

But I now know the day will come when I will find.

My True Queen that will want to always be mine.

One Love

I have to be honest I am not afraid as I once was in the past

Living in a lonely world my pride made me try to live life fast

So many of us search to find that one in our life

For me that True Queen that will one day be my wife

I can man up now and say that this is it for me

Life with all those others I could never come to see

I stand here now and say baby here I am

Us not being together was never a part of the plan

No worries I come with EveryRyThang that you need

You are the only one so it is time for me to concede

I reach out to you to take my hand

So that you always know that I am your man

The truth is you are all I need and I never want to let go

This was something made to last forever because I love you so

Soon we will be able to share our love with the man above

Then in our mind and heart we will know that this is all just One Love

©Joseph FbPoet Wilder2013

Not Better Than Me

I have been out here in these streets, and I have learned

That guy you give your loving to, does not need your
concern

He treats you like a substitute, and doesn't appreciate all
of your good

N doesn't give you all of the love, and respect that he
should

Never would think that he would bring you down to the
ground

Always want to act all cocky, just cus his boys come
around

But allow me to be your teacher, and I wont let you fall

With me by your side, you will always stand tall

He never understood you, so allow him to just be the past

I am playing for keeps, aint no planning on coming in last

I just need you to realize that with me is where I want you
to be

Cus whether here, or there regardless, Your Man Aint and
Wont Ever Be Better Than Me

©Joseph FbPoet Wilder 2014

Don't Leave

What we going to do right here is go back, way back, back into time

Before the tears, and frustration of wanting you to be mine

I have had my problems, and you have had yours too

But through it all, you are a queen that has remained true

If you take your love away from me, I will go insane

I will choose you always, over any fame

Searching for the words, to help you realize

That wanting you to stay, should have never been a surprise

Not just for a night, but I want you to stay close eveRyRday

But if you sail away, the center piece of me you will take away

By my side always, is where I would love for you to be

So please stay right here, and Don't Ever Leave Me

©Joseph FbPoet Wilder 2013

Comforter

I am going to need you to relax, lay down, and let me tell
you what is on my mind

I have held my feelings back long enough, not this time

Deep inside my heart, I feel that I made a very big mistake

But I am glad he did what he did, so that you could wake

Tired of seeing you cry, I can feel your pain

He has been casting too many shadows driving you insane

You can say, "Joe mind your business I am acting sensitive"

But I am always going to be there for you, while I live

To make you smile, knowing all the time that you are the
only one that I want to see

So now it is time for you to get up, and let that body come
Comfort Me

©Joseph FbPoet Wilder2013

Thinking bout You

We don't have to go to the party, just close your eyes, and
lets fly

I do not want you to leave, no time for a goodbye

You know what I am already thinking; you already did your
thang

So let me pull you closer, and you can get ready to sang

What I want is whether people are around, or not

Past the college days, already shut downdowndown the
Frat Spot

The chemistry that we share, I can feel is so true

So I will be the one to reach out, cus I am tired of just
Thinking Bout You!

©Joseph FbPoet Wilder 2013

Still N Love With You

Time passes so fast, but each day starts with my love for
you

You are the first one that I have known that has always
been true

I wont let my friends affect the happiness that we share

I am still the man for you that will always care

What else can I do to show you how much I love

In my heart what we have, I want to share with the man
above

You don't have to question; I am still yours, and only your
man

All that matters to me is that you are my biggest fan

To keep you happy is what I want, and choose to do

So smile my sexy baby, cus I am still The Man that is in
Love With You

©Joseph FbPoet Wilder2013

Sex Room

Its about to get real X-rated, so get ready to file your claim

You might need a couple of towels, for that I will take the blame

Hope you are ready for the workout, cus you are about to sweat

I will make a movie, so that we can have more than the mirrors
to reflect

I am going to grab your body, and not let go

Then we are going to get tangled up, from the bed down to the
flo

I hope you are ready to blast off, and then I can pull out your
inner freak

When I get my head underneath your leg, you won't be able to
speak

I am going to have you twisted, but it will be no need for a mat

But you are not going to stop leaking, as soon as I get close to
that cat

You can come with the T Shirt, and sexy panties, no need for a
costume

So how about you get to moving, and bring your ass to my Sex
Room

©Joseph FbPoet Wilder2013

To Know Her

All I can say is oooohhh bae, what did you do

Everybody has an addiction, mine just happens to be you

In the beginning you had your guard up, and I did too

We both were looking for a love, which was brand new

I never looked at you like you were a queen that needed to
be saved

Just someone in search for what they have craved

I cannot say that this is something that I have done before

You changed up the game, when you walked thru the door

A bond that we share, that goes beyond lust

I wanted to give you a love, which you could finally trust

With you in my life, I feel that I will always have my four
leaf clover

So all I can do is thank the Lord, for giving me the chance
to get to know her

©Joseph FbPoet Wilder 2013

Im Ready

I have something to say, and I am going to say right now.

No wondering I am going to give you a feeling that you never felt, if you allow.

This is something that I would hope that you never ignore.

Especially when you get that feeling that you never felt before.

Something so unthinkable, that feels so right.

So I will be the one to step up, and take the lead tonight.

I never want to give up, before we try.

We can take all of our love, and fly across the sky.

Then I can suspend you, in the air.

N show you, I already made the decision about how much I care.

So if you want I will go old school, and ask you to go steady.

But if you ask me, I am going to look into your eyes, and tell you that I am Ready!

©Joseph FbPoet Wilder2014

Love N Affection

It is time for me to make my own confession

But I do not want you to ever get the wrong impression

Desperate is not the way that I want to sound

But it is no longer time for us to fuc% around

Like a party to a dj, I always need you close to me

To be in your possession, is where I would luv to be

I want to feel your heartbeat when I hold u close

It is only you that I want to give me my special dose

We both are grown, so you need to let him know

That you are my world and this is our show

I tried to fight it off, but you are my special obsession

N it is only you that deserves my undivided attention

So I am ready to give you all of my Love and Affection

©Joseph FbPoet Wilder2014

Love N War

One day it will be only sunny skies I tell you no lie

We need to stop the madness, and never have to say
goodbye

When the fire starts, and we both prepare to explode

I never want us to have to come, to that crossroad

We both can go so hard, till we lose control

When you are the only one, which I want to console

To make it this far, for better or for worse

But at times, I feel like we have both been hit with a curse

After the smoke clears though, in my arms is where you
belong

On the frontline beside me standing so strong

The love that we share goes beyond just swag

For you I have no problem waving that flag

Even though the hurt, and pain neither of us will ever be
able to ignore

We have both accepted, that this is all just a part of Love N
War

©Joseph FbPoet Wilder 2013

35

Love You Down

Over time, it has never really mattered too much to me

Even though you are older, you are still my baby

My boo, my bae, no you will always be my queen which is true

The main character within my dream, helping me make it thru

It will never be a goodbye, only a goodnight

You are the only one, which I want to keep in my sight

I made the choice, and I want you to always stay around

So whatever it takes, I will make sure that I always Love You DownDownDown

©Joseph FbPoet Wilder 2013

Saved

She told me that she was hurting, and that she needed my help

A pain so deep, her heart has never felt

If I could assist her or if I knew someone that she could call

N I looked at her, and said that I will never let you fall

You don't have to look up in the sky for a bird or a plane

SuperMan, BatMan, SpiderMan, FbPoet, its all the same

No super trick here though, so please don't try to pull it

Cus I will bounce on you're a$$ real quick, like a speeding bullet

I told her that she needs to stop messing with brothas, just for riches

Then you won't get looked at negative, like these other b!tches

To not come looking for me to buy you a Dooney N Bourke

Cus when I was broke, you looked at me like it wouldn't work

Now I am here questioning, ah isa ah isa, should I save her

Is she even worth it, or should I defer

But she is my baby, and I won't let her ever be depraved

So just stay by my side, this way we can Both Be Saved!

©Joseph FbPoet Wilder2013

Wrong Places

Out of all of the days in my past, I bless the day that I found you

You set my heart on fire, because you are a Queen that is True

Had to learn with time, that it is nothing out there in those streets for me

Something for myself that I had to experience, and see

I take full responsibility for my past, and all of my ways

But with you by my side, is how I want to spend the rest of my days

You saw my needs, and thoughts, and changed my heart

With a true love that cared for me, from the start

At a time, when this man had nowhere to go

You stayed by my side, and said that I would never leave you Joe

That no matter the storm, I would never have to face it alone

She would stand with me, whether or not we have a throne

That I no longer need to be out there with others pleading cases

Cus all I have been doing is Looking for Love in All the Wrong Places!

©Joseph FbPoet Wilder2013

Imagine That

I don't want you to talk, baby let me take your mind into a zone

No cares in the world, I got this Daddys home

Take my hand, and lets go away

Just you, and me at this moment no more time to play

No worries right now, I just want you to relax

While I massage you all over, from front to back

This is something that I want you to divulge

All of your fantasies, I want you to indulge

Whip cream, strawberries, candles, and oils surrounding the bed

As I kiss all over your body from your feet to your head

Think about all of the sexual energy that we share

While you say my name, as I grab your hair

Stroking you so nice, not forgetting to lick the cat

So just let I go, close your eyes , N Just Imagine That!

©Joseph FbPoetWilder2013

Cant Stop Loving You

I can go back to the day that I met the perfect stranger

My mind had been made up, because of past danger

Felt like I was dying, until I saw the sun shining on you

Never thinking that at the same time, the Lord was blessing me too

At that moment you were just ready to argue, and fuss

Never knowing that at that time, it was all about the both of us

Our Love was calling, it did not matter the season

Then we looked into each other's eyes, and smiled without reason

I tried to tell myself, that I would never ever love another

Don't have any children, so was not looking for a mother

But I was not aware that Love was making a call

N I soon made the promise to never let her fall

With you it was no reason to ever tell a lie

To love you unconditionally came naturally, I didn't even have to try

My baby, My Love, My Heart, My Queen which is True

These are all of the reasons, Why I Cant Stop Loving You!

©Joseph FbPoet Wilder2013

Love Is Lost

Sitting here alone, all that I can do is reminisce

Oh how I long to hold you in my arms, and give you a kiss

Now that you are gone, I wonder what am I to do

I have never loved anyone, the way that I Love You

While you would lie in my arms, all that I could ever do was stare

Now that you have runaway, life just does not seem fair

When I close my eyes, and fall asleep you are all that I see

Feeling so lonely now that you are not with me

I was the one that was supposed to stay your king

What am I to do now without the wind beneath my wings

Now it feels as if I am constantly stuck in the rain

Cus us not together, feels insane

You can say that I never loved you like I should

But if you give me another chance I promise to do what I should

Never wanting to ever yearn for your touch

My True Queen that I realize that I love so much

Got me here now, stuck with the stupid face

Begging, and pleading while I try to make my case

But for you I don't care, and it does not matter the cost

Cus I refuse to go another day, feeling like my Love Is Lost

©Joseph FbPoet Wilder2014

You N I

It is time for me to tell you my story

Think it's a lie, ok then take me on Maury

I want to let you know, how it is that I feel

Im not trying to hold you, I wont make this too long

But the love that we share, is oh so strong

What we share, I never want to ever stop

I place you above all, you control the top

Not worried about others, it is you and me, me and you

More than making love, is what I want to do

A story we both live, that will never die

N that is why I want it to always remain, just You N I

©Joseph FbPoet Wilder2013

Missing You

Standing here looking out my window, with so much on my mind

You are the only one I wish, that I could find

EveRyRyday I have to stop myself from picking up the phone

But all I want, is for my baby to come back home

My nights are now long, and my days are so cold

Wanting the days back, when I had you to hold

With a heart so weak, at times I hallucinate

Should not have took so long, to try to articulate

Feel like the snow is now coming down in June

All I can do now, is try to sing you a tune

Like the desert, without the sand

Is how I feel, without your hand

Like a wedding without a groom

I never want you, to have to assume

That I am the one, that should have had a clue

That I cannot let you go, cus I'm Missing You!

©Joseph FbPoet Wilder2013

Want N Need

I want to believe that you can see my heart

Want us to be able to move on, and restart

I cannot let you leave me, and walk out the door

Your scars and tears I can no longer ignore

Wrong is all I have been, this I will admit

You gave me everything, and only asked me to commit

No more hoping. I already know that I have to right this wrong

Hoping that my mistake, will make us strong

Had to grow up, and let go of the old me

It took some time, but you are all that I want to see

Tired of being in the same place this I now know

Guess a King needed a lil dirt on me to be able to grow

You are the best part of my life

I refuse to lose my future wife

Yeah I said it, that's what I said

We need to finish this race, and go get wed

The stakes are now way too high, so I will take the lead

So will you please take my hand, cus you are all I Want N Need!

©Joseph FbPoet Wilder2013

Just Like That

Tired of hearing you ask, so if you really wanna know

I'm going to slow it down a sec, and take it real slow

I would like to take this time, to explain my joy

It's Like a child on Christmas, when they are opening up their new toy

Like when you finally hear, your baby's first word

Like when you know in your heart, your man won't be deterred

Like sitting by the fire place, in the winter time

Like taking a moment, to even understand this rhyme

Like when you are down, and I make you feel alright

Like a fool moon, as it shines bright at night

Like sitting in a small café, while I hold you in my arms

Like when we are together, you know it won't be any harm

Like breaking up, then having makeup sex

Like when we don't make things so d@mn complex

Like when the storm comes, and the shelter keeps us safe

Like when we look into each other's eyes n cut that cake

My baby that I love, I need no other names in the hat

So If you really wanna know how I Feel, Ooooooooohh Just Like That!

©Joseph FbPoet Wilder2013

Do Me Baby

Here we are the two of us, looking for a reason

Starring each other down, it never mattered the season

I want you just as bad, as you want me

But to take this long, is not the way that it is supposed to be

Until the war is over, I refuse to stop

While we switch different positions, from the bottom to the top

To touch, and kiss you all over, you never have to ask

I want to listen to you grown, as I complete this task

When you do what you do, I can never love no other

So I have no problem, if you put your queen on my face, and
smother

I need, n want your love, like never before

So give it to me baby, till I just can't take no more

No need for you to worry, I am never trying to tease

This is not a dream, I'm going to make sure that I please

All I want to hear is YES Baby Yes, It will be no maybe

So get you a$$ over here right now, N Do Me Baby

©Joseph FbpPoet Wilder2013

Weekend Love

Just waiting for someone to say, that you are in town

I often think about how I love when you were around

Always wanting you here next to me

A dream that I once again need to see

Waiting for the morning when I awake with you by my side

You here with me, someone that I can always confide

After all of this time, I still do not want you to ever leave

You serve a special part of me, cus you always believed

It will always be more than a memory that we share

The love that we have, no one else can ever compare

While I thank the Lord, for our love that will always
continue to begin

I will let you know now, that I want to love you for more
than just a Weekend

©Joseph FbPoet Wilder2013

One More Night

The time has come, in which we both need to Learn

My focus is only us; others do not have my concern

Trying so long to let you know how I feel

Wondering if I should just call, and keep it real

No plan on Stumbling, I have already fallen for you

If you sail away, I don't know what I will do

Hoping, and Praying, that you change your mind

For I know that your Love, is one of a kind

But time is not on our side, and I Refuse to wait

I don't want to ever feel, like I am too late

Like a river to the sea, I will stay by your Side

You are the only one that I want to Confide

So I will prepare myself, but I do not want us to ever again
Fight

But Please, I am going to need you to give me of A Lot
more than just One More Night!

©Joseph FbPoet Wilder2013

Only One for Me

I have seen too many things that turned out too good to
be true

Like when you find out, the joke has always been on you

Just wanting to be the best man that I can

So to come straight from my heart is the plan

I want you always, and can't let go

To never hurt, and lie to you, I want you to know

All I can ever do, is to show you how

My better judgment, has opened up my heart now

Only truth, I can't look at you, and lie threw my teeth

To never let you fall, I promise to always be underneath

Now I am waiting, for you to just come around

If you give me half a chance, you will have found

That I will be the man that you need me to be

You just need to open up your eyes, and see

That you will always be, the Only One for ME!

©Joseph FbPoet Wilder2013

Like I Love You

As the clock strikes all I can do is sit, and wonder why

How could I allow you to leave, and say goodbye

Trying to grasp a understanding, of what to do

Always knowing that I should have never tried to deceive you

Going crazy, I now don't know what to think

Never thought that I would be the one to blink

I would like to say that I was just going thru a phase

Now I can't live without you, and wish for better days

I know that I have to do what it takes, to keep you here with me

I have faith that you will someday see

That I never met a queen that made me feel like it was time

Who we got to fu%k up baby, my lil partner in crime

But I realize that you should never want to be with a man

Especially If he is one, that does not make you a part of his plan

So all I can do is hope that you see that my words for you are
True

Cus I'm telling you now, that He Can't Love You like I Love You!

Joseph FbPoet Wilder2013

Always Love You

Every day, and night it is you that consumes my mind

The memory that I have for you is one of a kind

Trying to find a pathway, back to you

So I can help with all of your special wishes coming true

Into many pieces, I have already been broken down

But my love for you, will always be around

24/7 I will remain the very best

This night I will be your treasure, I confess

When things go wrong, I will always be there to assist

You wont need to close your eyes n even make a wish

To Hold You, Day N Night, Night N Day

EveRy waking moment I want you to stay

Cus you are my heart, N my love for you is true

N I want you to know, That I Will Always Love You!

©Joseph FbPoet Wilder2013

All I Need

I remember back in the day, when I used to eat sardines for dinner.

Coming up in this cold world, I was just a beginner.

Wanting to be paid, and to shine in that lime light.

Till I realized what I needed to make it thru the night.

If you don't know, then now you should know.

You are the star that is stealing this show.

The only one that has my heart.

It has been all on you from the start.

I don't want nobody else, all I need is you.

You already know who you are, My Queen that is True!

From the beginning, it has all been a dream.

The only one that I need on my team.

Now I ask you, to put it all on me.

Without you, is something I don't want to see.

True words from my mouth, never trying to stunt.

Cus You ARE THE ONLY ONE that I Need N Want!

©Joseph FbPoet Wilder2013

Womans Work

I share my thoughts, this is never a joke

I pray to God, that you will be able to cope

To cry I should, but I can't let it show

Always thought that our love, would be able to grow

Tired of hoping, but I always continue to think

Want the moments back that I chose to blink

All the things I should've said that I never said

This goes deeper than just getting wed

The little kisses that I miss so much

But our love went beyond any physical touch

More than just holding your pretty lil hand

I was happy just to say I was your man

Now I want this pain to just go away

Your love child needs your love to stay

With you by my side, was my own special perk

So nothing is over, cus I refuse to give up on this Woman's Work!

©Joseph FbPoet Wilder2014

Every Beat of My Heart

I ask that you clear your mind, and just relax.

Take my hand, and know I will always have your back.

My words I share, I want you to know today.

It will be no need to fear, cus I want you to stay.

Does not matter if you are from Jupiter, and I am from Mars.

As long as we are together underneath these stars

No need to worry, so you can close your eyes.

N tomorrow will be better, no negative surprise.

When I come thru the door, it no longer will be time to play.

More than just my words will take your breath away.

But you are so many miles away N, I hate for us to be apart.

But Regardless, this Day, I am still going to Luv You with EveRyRy Beat of My Heart!!!

©Joseph FbPoet Wilder2014

Love N Affection

I don't want you to ever get the wrong impression.

If you want to leave, it has always been your discretion.

L. O. V. E. is what I want; I hope I am not sounding too desperate.

I just never want you to turn around, and choose to exit.

I will moan your name, so that you know you are in control.

Gripping you so tight is how I want to hold.

As I gently kiss your forehead, as I lay you down.

Moving like thieves in the night, while I lick n poke you all around.

I can give you what you want, and you can give me what I need.

I can be stingy if you like, and always take the lead.

But I won't slip, and that means you are not going to fall.

Well, maybe when I have you screaming, up against the wall.

Not worried if I am the one that is on your mind.

I know you can't get past that vision, of me hitting it from behind.

But I hope you know that I am talking about more, than just a physical connection.

Cus to keep My Attention,

I am going to Need ALL of Your Love N Affection!!!

©Joseph FbPoet Wilder2014

Wait for My Love

In life we will learn that certain things are true.

Things don't always work out the way that you would like them to.

I never want to stop believing that it could someday be.

That special bond, shared between just you, and me!

But I can't dream, and continue to waste time.

Wishing, and hoping that someday you will be mine.

See in my head the picture is now finally clear

For it is you that I want to always stay near

Remembering a time not too long ago, always having a lonely heart

Wanting the love I been missing, is where I would like to start

If you didn't know, I am telling you now that this is fate.

I never want to feel that we waited too late.

But I know that things take time, and I do not want to rush

Just hard to do when you are the one that I miss so much.

All that I can ask for is to be given the chance

To give you All of My Love, N Special Romance

For it has already been said N done from the Man Above.

Letting you know, that you should Never have to Wait for Any of My Love!

©Joseph FbPoet Wilder2014

Always Love

Most thought that we would never last

But those are ones that never supported our cast

Always knowing that eventually we would get there someday

The Only One I want, in my life to stay

Us being together, is where we both belong

Sharing a unbreakable bond, that is oh So Strong

For me, you will never have to run

My love for you has already begun

No need to worry if this is just a dream

You are the Only One that I want on our team

I say Ours, because you are a part of the story now

The Only One that I want to share a vow

N to just hold close, and to kiss at night

N to look into your eyes, and let know that things will be alright

Together the odds we both will beat

To love you how you deserve, and to never mistreat

Cus I am Your King, and I place no one else above

For You Are The Only One, that I will Always Love!!!

©Joseph FbPoet Wilder2014

Choosey Lover

I will tell you a story, not too long ago

Imma need you to keep up, no time to be acting slow

Always kidding myself that she would be true

Something that I thought MY BABY, would always do

She had my love, She knew what she had earned

Had me looking stupid, in time I learned

But Not You, My Baby Yo te quiero aqui

Im telling you Right Now, I Want You Here With Me!!!

Your decision, has made me more than glad

No need to tell you, you are the best I've had

Over time you have proven what you said

You knew things went Deeper, than just getting you in bed

Standing by my side, with all of the security you have gave

Your last worry, is that I will ever miss-behave

I am so proud of you, that you took the chance, to finally
discover

That it worked out for you in the long run, to be a CHOOSEY
LOVER!!!!!

©Joseph FbPoet Wilder2014

Shivering N Shaking

Wait for It, Wait for it, cus tonight you are going to scream.

I am going to have you feeling, like you are stuck in a dream.

No need to guess, what it is that I am trying to do.

When I look into your eyes, you are going to get a clue.

I don't play NO games, you already know that I am sick with my tongue!

You will be screaming my name, after it gets flung,.

I will let you feel all of this Jacuzzi jet.

You will be more than woozy after I get you wet.

No need to worry, I will always keep my composer.

While I start from your forehead, to your chest, then flip ya, and fold ya.

We don't need any cameras, but a movie we will shoot.

I hope you are ready to dribble, when I taste that fruit.

You are going to take every inch, until you start to shiver.

While I make my way DownDownDown, your flowing river!

Your own special lil paradise, you will have found.

You are going to be happy, that you decided to keep me around.

My focus is on you, not concerned on making a baby.

Im just happy right now, to say that you are my lady.

It will be No need to even think, that she may be faking.

Cus im going to bust it wide open, N have that Leg Shivering N Shaking!!!

©Joseph FbPoet Wilder2014

Come Back 2 Me

The Lord already knows that I have tried

He has felt my pain, and knows that I have cried

Always wanting to just live our life as one

Never wanted it to be just a hit, and run

All my life I have waited, for a Queen that is True

The tough times, I always thought I could make it thru

Just Hold On, He is getting Her right for you my friends would say

But that was so long ago, didn't think I would still be waiting today

After all of this time, it is I that cannot let go

For it is you that I want, this I hope that you know

Had to learn the feeling, of an abandoned heart

Never thought I would be begging you now, can we please restart

You are comprised of a full package, that NoOne else can compare

For you are a True Queen, which is now so rare

Was forced to learn, the whole point of give and take

N whose face it is that I wish to see, when I awake

Cus your beautiful smile, is what I again wish to feel, and see

So I Am Asking My Love, Can You Please Come Back To Me???

©Joseph FbPoet Wilder2014

Broken Road

It is one thing that I know is true

That ya boy is very versatile too

Long ago I set out on that narrow road

Looking for My True Queen that I could someday hold

But thru the trial n tribulations at times I got lost

For divine true happiness comes with a cost

Queens from my past allowed me to be directed on my way

Like the North Star let my people know, they would be free someday

All my long lost dreams always make me reminisce

Oh how I wish for all of life's bliss

I ask that you smile and take my hand

I already know the truth, I hope you understand

Will admit that I did not pay attention to the signs

To respect what I had, I had to be blind

But I know it is a grander plan, this much is true

For the Broken Road has already been Blessed for Me N You!!

©Joseph FbPoet Wilder2014

Drunk N Love

Eat the cake Anna Mae, and take one more sip

I'm going to slip them panties to the side, once those pants I
unzip

Allow me to take your body to new heights

Won't be a charge, once when we make our flashing lights

As I lay you down, and your body starts to swerve

Then rub, and kiss all of your sexy curves

I will not leave an inch of your body un-explored

I'm going to let you ride the wave, on this surf board

I only want my fatty, it will be no complaints

Fucking around with me, you are going to stumble in faint

I Only speak truth, Me, MySelf, N I, must say

When you awake, it will be such a brighter day

Baby I want you, with a camera or not

Got me like a wild animal, oh so hot

Complete satisfaction will come with all of thee above

So no need to guess, I am definitely going to have you Drunk in
Love!!!!

©Joseph FbPoet Wilder2014

Politics

I watch all news including Fox to try to understand.

The rights agenda and their ultimate plan.

I try not to blame those who are white.

But most of them don't know who they want to fight.

We all to some degree follow things good and bad.

But most don't know that we all have been had.

Indians, Blacks, Oriental, Hispanics, now Arabs.

Have all been used but that is not what is sad.

It is the Caucasians in the same boat as you and I.

That the right uses now to try to get by.

They complain about illegal's, deficits, but ultimately a black man at the top.

But if you believe he is the one running things you really need to stop.

We all need to look in the mirror and make a Change.

But the right wants you to get that gun and go to the range.

Now speaking as a brotha from the South Side of the Chi that knows the street.

Trust when I say there are a lot of brothas you don't wanna meet.

So keep listening to Palin, Colter, Hannity, Rush, and all the rest.

But remember that you are the ones that asked for this test.

©Joseph FbPoet Wilder2013

Health Care

Used to hate on Michigan now Wisconsin has caught my eye

Yall have let the Right just tell one big lie

I say a lie because Walker could/should not have won

But what am I to say if it has already been said n done

Red states Blue states but we are supposed to stand hand n hand

N yall can't even come to an agreement to make a health care plan

I can't honor any of it now cus too much special interest is involved

But most can't even see that we have all already been blackballed

I ASK what does that Annuit Coeptus mean to you??

N to get it do you just take it or do what you got to do

Have you gotten to that point where that defines who you are

Or have you awakened amongst the shining few other stars

My problem is I want all to see or just engage n the lil that I know

But EveRyRyBody isn't going to sit down n be quiet till after the beginning of the show

So I will keep it simple n just say that we have pissed Momma off real bad

N No song Today cus this Sh!t is just too d@mn SAD

©Joseph FbPoet Wilder2013

Hot in Here

Republicans say that Reagan did not raise taxes, and the economy did good

But isn't that the same time that they let crack hit the hood

Of course they were paid, and people were hustling in the street

But with the incarceration rate, we now know that was a plan set in motion for defeat

Then they argue about God, Jerusalem, and Israel's fate

Didn't the forefathers say that they wanted to separate church, and state

Like the only way that you can get to heaven is if you vote for the right

The party known for using only their ears for sight

With health care, you just better have a magical cape

N if you are a queen, it is now your fault if you are raped

Are we supposed to get our news from fox

The station where EveRyRyBody is still smoking rocks

Being so religious, you would think that they would understand the word hope

But what can you expect, from the party that introduced the world to dope

All they do is continue to make those on the right look slow

N ultimately everyone nonwhite should be considered a foe

What is the problem with the top% putting their fair share in the hat

Then maybe you can say that we did Help Build That

A party of no individuals, cus Grover Norquist has set fear

So we better all get ready, cus it definitely about to really get hot in here

©Joseph FbPoet Wilder2013

Do You

This world is crazy; I just thought that you should know

I am not the smartest, but I am never slow

With life you have to learn how to decipher the bull

Cus it will always be those that try to pull that wool

Like with politics it is funny how when we had Clinton they
were banging in Lil Rock

Now we get Obama, and you see kids murdered in the Chi
on eVeRy block

With relationships people are no longer serious they just
pass the time

EveRyRybody trying to figure out what is going on in
someone else's mind

With religion it is so much we are right, and you are wrong

EveRyRybody wanna feel like they are the only ones who
belong

But I cannot, and don't want to control what it is that you
are trying to do

As long as it doesn't in ANY way negatively affect me
continue to do you

©Joseph FbPoet Wilder2013

What's Going On

We are told that in the US we have freedom of speech

But it all really boils down to what you are trying to teach

They wonder why blacks are mad about this horrific trial

We on the other hand try to figure out why they live in denial

All of this negativity was just a slap in the face

Because it appears that neither side really brought a good case

But beyond this case, African Americans across this country feel that we are treated unfair

What we deal with on a daily basis, other races can't even compare

We are stuck in the fifties, but at least then our community stood together strong

But now most are so focused on the bull, just trying to belong

It is no question to us the outcome, had this been the other way around

The book would have been thrown; they wouldn't have even considered stand your ground

I guess this is their way of promoting carry and conceal

But what happened to throwing them thangs, to seal that deal

To my brothas in the street I hope that we all wake up and see

Cus What's Going On Now is not the way that it is supposed to be

©Joseph FbPoet Wilder2014

Where is the Love

I want to take this time, and talk about the world today

Even though I know that most, won't take the time to even read what I have to say

We had to deal first with Trayvon Martin, now Jonathan A. Ferrell , a whole other case

But we must practice what we preach, cus this goes beyond just race

Bloods, Crips, Moes, Folks, Kings, N Lords

Can't act like the KKK is the only ones out here pulling those swords

People killing each other eveRyRyday, making all cry

Mothers are the ones now, having to tell their babies goodbye

But this goes beyond just talking about the good U.S. of A.

This is not Saturday Night Live, I'm not talking about Tina Fey

The world as a whole carries all of the negative weight

Chemical bombs are now being dropped because of all the hate

But the media on all sides have to add their spin

They try to control your mind before you even try to begin

It's known if they control your mind, the truth you will never know

N after a while would be attracted to all of the drama flow

Now most don't have any values for humanity

They only care about money, which causes Vanity

Main reason why at times I feel blue

Cus not just my race, but none of us have a clue

I would love to believe that we are all one

That goes beyond whether or not you believe in the Father N Son

But to divide, and conquer has always been the plan

It was seen before that if we worked together we could make a stand

This goes beyond government; this is something that individuals must decide

It's not about money, race, or wealth, and all of that pride

I would hope that my words touch you, take it as a sign from the Man Above

Cus the question that we all should be asking each other, Is Where Is the Love?

Respect

Had to write some words for Mandela, President of South Africa, which was wrongfully imprisoned!

But I must First be honest, and talk about my crazy vision

I am not going to lie, me as a Black Man never gave him the respect that he deserved.

I only knew the general information, from what I may have read or heard.

Yes I am dogging me, but we all are the ones at fault

We don't give the honor to those that for us to have a better future always fought!

This man was in jail for over 27 years, for trying to help us ALL

He wasn't out there just having a lil Town Hall!

This goes beyond FB, Tweeting Etc. just trying to get across your message

This Man ended Apartheid, and provided a whole country with leverage!

So yes, in myself I am upset, that so much information I chose to neglect

But I feel that I must be honest in order to give my full respect

©Joseph FbPoet Wilder2014

Aware

Let's look at the tax problem that we have at hand

It all really boils down to supply, and demand

The right thinks that less taxes means more products that they can supply

The Left understands that no one will have the money for their products to buy

The whole process now is just one big mess

Cus the majority of people are the ones that are receiving less

Both sides convey a message that is hard to understand

You can't even get the truth so that you can come up with a plan

This side says this, and this side says that

But which side wants to ultimately contribute money to the hat

Messages for both parties now have too much spin

Just want you to see it their way, something only FOX could begin

No President decides or makes policy by himself, he has to work with the congress he was dealt

So how can it be any progress if for the last 4yrs Republicans didn't offer any help

To understand it, the distinguished gentlemen is a movie that you should rent

You will learn that nothing can be done without the few elites consent

How can they pay 13% and I pay almost thirty

Then they want to look at me like I am all needy, and dirty

I guess that it is too much to think this world can be fair

But I am still going to do my best to make sure those in and out THE GHETTO are aware

©Joseph FbPoet Wilder2015

71

Change

What is it in life that we all know that we share

No matter when or where you have awaken it has always been there

Besides you it has always been mother earth

She has been there regardless since you were first given birth

We have raped her long enough n have attacked her blood line

Whether we have drilled for oil or dug for coal n a mine

Big money will make you think that it is nothing n all is alright

N that we can continue on this same path, and make it thru the night

They will make you think that racism past n present never did exist

Just like the story of Willie Lynch over time they knew that you would soon forget

Have us turn against each other, and hopes that we will not know who to blame

N we fall for it hook line n sinker n we should all be ashamed

The all Seeing Eye has always kept its eye on each one of us

A one world order to the elite has always been a must

To keep us separated over time so that we could never have a voice

But allow us to elect officials who would then make our choice

The differences that we share stem from our divisions not understanding where it is that each has come from

But we all have been waiting a long long time but I still have faith that A Change Still Gone Come

©Joseph Wilder2014

Started at the Bottom

Must I remind you; how quick it is that most forget the past.

Started at the bottom, and we still come in last.

We say, "yes sir master" still everyday.

May not pick that cotton, but taxes etc. we still pay.

EBT, Link, Section 8, yes we need however it is still a handout.

Just like when Masser only gave slaves chitterlings to put in their mouth.

Think about that for a sec., the inner intestines comprised of Sh!t.

That smell, and odor that I will never forget.

But those slaves in the past made it work, and did what they had to do.

Sad part now, most act like they don't have a clue.

Look at your dollar bill, that Novus Ordos Seclurum has always been there.

Or maybe when it comes to that New World Order you don't really care.

That annuit coeptis is now all that is on people's mind.

So for that American Tender, people will sale their behind.

These people fought, and died just so that we could have a vote.

Now most act confused, like they just got off the boat.

Oh, we have a Black President, so u think all is cool?

If you think that he is running sh!t, lol then you are the fool.

I understand that life is hard, and most times not fair.

Why do you think Republicans are so mad about Obama Care?

My grandmother love you Mae Lee, who just turned a 103.

Still remembers seeing her friends hanging in a tree.

I know most don't care, and try not to understand.

But maybe that is why African Americans will always be looked at as 3/5 of a man!!

Religion

Most will never understand, and I don't want to ever feel my pain

I share my words in hope that you will have something positive to gain

The truth of the matter is they're lessons that I have had to learn

Even though I know that most in this world, don't have a concern

It has been times that I have cried, and could not see

Until I was told that I have to Let It Go, Let It Be

It is not about rubies, diamonds, silver, or pearls

The true glory we cannot trade in for anything in this world

All of my calculated blessing from the beginning to the end

Goes a lot deeper than just a like, from a FB friend

One of these days I am going to have all I want but more importantly
All that I Need

This goes beyond any type of selfish greed

To be loved more than I have ever known

N to have the promise that I will never be left alone

Words from my mouth, that I will always decree

For I know that His Will is what is best for me!

Joseph FbPoet Wilder2014

Friend N Jesus

Can we find a friend so faithful all our pain and sorrow
they share

That knows our every weakness and how we are
cumbered with a load of care

We must all get ready for the miracle to come

N that does not matter where it is the message comes
from

I stand before you now n put my name on it

My God has a blessing for me that I will never forget

I will take back all the devil has taken from me

I won't and cannot go back to the way that things used to
be

The devil has already begun to up his attack

But he was already defeated and would like to come back

We have already won that is what the devil wants to take

He will kill, lie, steal and is always fake

We must commit to the Father and have complete trust

N know that we all will always Have a Friend in Jesus

©Joseph FbPoet Wilder2014

My Poem

Only you are my heart's desire

Thru you I use my words to try to inspire

This is my poem this is my song

While I praise my savior all day long

He only is my strength and my rock

With the lord is where I place all of my stock

Within God is my salvation and all of my glory

Never ever forgetting his mercy according to His Story

We all must learn how to keep the good and the bad apart

You should never let oppression or money sit on your heart

God is my joy, sorrow, hope, He is my EveryRyThang

It is a deeper love we share never just a fling

We must understand and learn how important is favor

Then you will be able to trust and love your neighbor

But we all have to learn the difference between lust and
unconditional love

Then we will be able to understand the supernatural of the man
above

©Joseph FbPoet Wilder2015

Say Yes

With an upright man, thou will show thyself upright.

But you must keep the righteousness, always in your sight.

We all will lose sight from time to time. But it is always
another story, so we cannot be blind.

We should never be so quick to judge at all.

That might be the reason, that we miss our call

We are taught, to search for the Lord forever more.

But we cannot be afraid, to answer the knock at the door.

We have to realize all good, and bad happen for a reason.

But to receive the product, we have to endure the whole
season.

The devil will try to trick us, from what it is that we need to
do

So I now Say Yes to You always since You have always been
True.

©Joseph FbPoet Wilder 2013

He's Able

Tragedy can be found in a common place.

It doesn't depend on stature, class, creed, or race.

You have to remember that He is able.

And that is truth not a fable.

We all in time can go through a drought.

You just have to understand what this is all about.

See people are afraid of church because of restrictions.

But He was wounded and bruised for our transgressions.

So don't give up on God cus He won't give up on you.

He is able to do all that he said that he will do.

©Joseph FbPoet Wilder2015

Near

Just the other day, I heard a man say.

He didn't believe in Gods Word but I can say today.

We have to remember that the lord has made a way.

See today you have to know is history.

And tomorrow will try to be a mystery.

You have to be more concerned with your life than making a living. Because it is more about giving than receiving.

Man can be self-centered and will need to feed his ego.

Because when we fail it is hard to sometimes let go.

But the one thing that we must all know.

That you must make yourself a servant unto all that you might grow.

You must have the courage to continue without fear.

And realize what is important that we should always keep near.

©Joseph FbPoet Wilder2015

Sweetest Thing I Know

The devil will always take you farther than you want to go.

And will try his best to steal the show.

We learn with time the clock has no dominion.

And that is fact not an opinion.

Sometimes the scraps are better than the main course.

And the lord shall always be your main source.

When it seems like the sun will not shine.

God can put a rainbow just to remind.

To save deliver set free and heal.

You have to give permission so that you can feel.

So remember you are a blessing that's what the word said.

And if riches increase don't get your heart on it and let it go to your head. Because the name Jesus is the sweetest thing I know.

And that is something I will never ever be afraid to show.

©Joseph FbPoet Wilder2015

Various

What catches my attention first, I would have to say shoes.

It lets me know in the door if I will be feeling the blues,

Is this queen versatile can she change her style

Or does baby girl look like she has been walking some miles.

I understand everyRythang yes everyRythang has its time and place.

But if the shoe game not tight every ry thang yes every ry thang else is a waste.

Make It

We all think that we have it bad.

Like we are the only one who at times gets sad.

You never know what hand that you may be given.

All you can do is stay positive and keep on living.

If I could, I wish that I could save us all.

Every Ry Body Yes Every Ry D@mn body would never fall.

I have faith that one day I will get my wish.

And no one ever again we will have to miss.

I know some really choose not to care.

But you can't then turn around and say that life isn't fair.

Every Ry Thang yes every ry thang in this world does not
revolve around just you.

So it will take a combined effort of us all if we want to
make it thru.

©Joseph FbPoet Wilder2013

Thank you

I want to take this time to show my appreciation to all

Whether you are a new friend or been around before I had my fall

I write to clear my head and to help others day

But I understand there are some that don't understand what I am trying to say

Even to those that push me to utilize my talent to get paid

Down to the ones that even think I'm just trying to get laid

When people meet me they say you cut and sexy (ThankYou) but you look bigger on your page

But trust the LiL Bandit will shut it downdowndown on or off the stage

Some say I still cant believe that you don't have a child

Which is easy to me, a lot of queens out here are too d@mn wild

I post and over time I have learned a lot

Like the key words that seem to make most women hot

Marriage, Wife, Love, and when I am nasty Lick

Just still waiting for someone to stand on it and claim this ???k

Let me stop now before I start to go off line

So I say Thank You to ALL for appreciating my clean, yet dirty mind!!!

©Joseph FbPoet Wilder2013

You's a Hoe

The question is what is your definition of a hoe?

Cus it appears I might be wrong, but most don't really know!

Is the action done so that you may benefit your seeds?

Or is it done just so that you can satisfy your needs?

Do you act like all is sweet, and your actions don't count?

Or do you just let the brothers get on top of you, and mount?

Can your actions later cause any harm to another??

What do you think would be said by your own mother???

Have you let your past define who you are now?

Are you always ready to drop on your knees, and bow???

Do you feel that eveRyRybody around you has something, to
you that is owed?

Or maybe you can't determine who is an associate, family,
friend, or foe!

Maybe I put too much confidence, and in the end you really
don't know!

So no need to guess anymore, you should already know that
You's A Hoe!!!!!

Joseph FbPoet Wilder2013

Best of Both Worlds

With me you can have a lil bit of all sides

Ya boy from the Chi is where I reside

Never Michael Jordan, but my words I do own

So you can let me know when you want me to take you home

I always will have hatters, but don't think that I won't make it to the top

I am more than a Sexy BodiaAAAaaAAaa, and won't be stopped

The motorcycle tried, but couldn't hold me down

Crept back into the game, and didn't even make a sound

Don't need a million on that boy writing; regardless I will shut downdowndown the place

Just waiting on you to decide when you want to give me more than a taste

Or that you know that I want you to be more than just my girl

Cus with me, you definitely will always get the best of both worlds

©Joseph FbPoet Wilder 2013

SuperMan

Some look, and the FbPoet is all that they see

Others say that you are just plain old Joey to me

Regardless, no one can speak on my behalf

Especially those that want what they can't have

Had to learn not to let another b!tch bring me down

Why would a brotha even want to join you on the ground

But it is one thing that I will always Know

Monday thru Sunday, they want to all steal the show

I don't want you to get me wrong, I love dem hoes

That crazy thing in life, just the way it goes

Most can guess what it is that I am talking about

Others, it doesn't bother me if you choose to walk out

I would hope that you don't want me to save you girl

That's that crazy sh!t that makes a brotha wanna earl

Not about to buy you a ring like Kobe's wife

But I can still make you a Celebrity over night

Don't call me fake, if so you really don't know Joe

Never a jealous man, always your choice to go

Don't wanna put anthrax on the tampax, I have betters ways to make it where you can't
stand

But maybe I will luv you oneday, but right now, a brotha not trying to be your
SuperMannnnn!

©Joseph FbPoet Wilder2014

Freaks of the Industry

Well they say that birds do it, and bees do it as well

I'm just waiting on you to give me a chance to ring that bell

Im not a heavy weight but I will go twelve rounds

So with a jab and a stick I will lick you up, and down

I will nibble around your ears, before I suck up on your neck

Making sure that I please all of you, no time for neglect

Oh Lil Bandit you will be screaming, while I take you home

While I hit it, lick it, and split as long as you condone

Don't need Vanessa Del Rio, no need for a snapper

I just want my nasty girl, whose booty is a clapper

With my head under her arm, under her leg, under my toe

We can take it fast if you want, or break it down real slow

It will never be a question if this is sex, just fu(%ing, or even love

When we get together you already know that it will be all of
thee above

But actions speak louder than words, and you will soon see

That retirement time is now over, for the Freak of the Industry

©Joseph FbPoet Wilder 2013

Im A King

A thank you that I send always to the man above

It is just funny to me though how much people are willing
to share

A lot post it all, and don't even care

I want others to like, respect my words, and not to hate

But I am still confident, and don't need anyone else to
validate

Then there are those that post bogus grown pics of their
children like that is cute

So you shouldn't be surprised when in a few years they are
ready to bear that fruit

Not trying to come off bogus, and sound all mean

Or to down any of you, and to sh!t on your dream

But I'm just letting all know right now, that the heat your
boy is about to bring

N if you didn't already know, That Boy Right There!

Yeah He A King!

©Joseph FbPoet Wilder2013

Wanna Be Saved

She told me that she was hurting, and that she needed my help

A pain so deep, her heart has never felt

If I could assist her or if I knew someone that she could call

N I looked at her, and said that I will never let you fall

You don't have to look up in the sky for a bird or a plane

SuperMan, BatMan, SpiderMan, FbPoet, its all the same

No super trick here though, so please don't try to pull it

Cus I will bounce on you're a$$ real quick, like a speeding bullet

I told her that she needs to stop messing with brothas, just for riches

Then you won't get looked at negative, like these other b!tches

To not come looking for me to buy you a Dooney N Bourke

Cus when I was broke; you looked at me like it wouldn't work

Now I am here questioning, ah isa ah isa, should I save her

Is she even worth it, or should I defer

But she is my baby, and I won't let her ever be depraved

So just stay by my side, this way we can Both Be Saved!

©Joseph FbPoet Wilder2013

Wrong Places

Out of all of the days in my past, I bless the day that I found you

You set my heart on fire, because you are a Queen that is True

Had to learn with time, that it is nothing out there in those streets for me

Something for myself that I had to experience, and see

I take full responsibility for my past, and all of my ways

But with you by my side, is how I want to spend the rest of my days

You saw my needs, and thoughts, and changed my heart

With a true love that cared for me, from the start

At a time, when this man had nowhere to go

You stayed by my side, and said that I would never leave you Joe

That no matter the storm, I would never have to face it alone

She would stand with me, whether or not we have a throne

That I no longer need to be out there with others pleading cases

Cus all I have been doing is Looking for Love in All the Wrong Places!

©Joseph FbPoet Wilder2013

Imagine That

I don't want you to talk, baby let me take your mind into a zone

No cares in the world, I got this Daddys home

Take my hand, and let's go away

Jus you, and me at this moment no more time to play

No worries right now, I just want you to relax

While I massage you all over, from front to back

This is something that I want you to divulge

All of your fantasies, I want you to indulge

Whip cream, strawberries, candles, and oils surrounding the bed

As I kiss all over your body from your feet to your head

Think about all of the sexual energy that we share

While you say my name, as I grab your hair

Stroking you so nice, not forgetting to lick the cat

So just let I go, close your eyes, N Just Imagine That!

©Joseph FbPoetWilder2013

Missing You

Standing here looking out my window, with so much on my mind

You are the only one I wish, that I could find

EveRyRyday I have to stop myself from picking up the phone

But all I want, is for my baby to come back home

My nights are now long, and my days are so cold

Wanting the days back, when I had you to hold

With a heart so weak, at times I hallucinate

Should not have took so long, to try to articulate

Feel like the snow is now coming down in June

All I can do now, is try to sing you a tune

Like the desert, without the sand

Is how I feel, without your hand

Like a wedding without a groom

I never want you, to have to assume

That I am the one, that should have had a clue

That I cannot let you go, cus I'm Missing You!

©Joseph FbPoet Wilder2013

Crazy Crazy Crazy

With time I finally realized the wrong that I have done

I have been a fool for too long, just wanting to have fun

All I can ask, is that my baby please stay

If I can't see you again, I don't know if I can last another
day

I know that lately it seems that all I do is apologize

But when you ran away from me, it was a horrible surprise

Just wanting to hold you, and to be able to once again see
your face

My True Queen that I love, and never want to replace

With a loss for words, I now can't even think

Always worried about others, when I was the one who
blinked

But for you I want more, and refuse to be lazy

Cus without you in my life, I will be CrazyCrazyCrazy

©Joseph FbPoet Wilder2013

Do Me Baby

Here we are the two of us, looking for a reason

Starring each other down, it never mattered the season

I want you just as bad, as you want me

But to take this long, is not the way that it is supposed to be

Until the war is over, I refuse to stop

While we switch different positions, from the bottom to the top

To touch, and kiss you all over, you never have to ask

I want to listen to you grown, as I complete this task

When you do what you do, I can never love no other

So I have no problem, if you put your queen on my face, and smother

I need, n want your love, like never before

So give it to me baby, till I just can't take no more

No need for you to worry, I am never trying to tease

This is not a dream, I'm going to make sure that I please

All I want to hear is YES Baby Yes, It will be no maybe

So get you a$$ over here right now, N Do Me Baby

©Joseph FbpPoet Wilder2013

One More Night

The time has come, in which we both need to Learn

My focus is only us; Others do not have my concern

Trying so long to let you know how I feel

Wondering if I should just call, and keep it real

No plan on Stumbling, I have already fallen for you

If you sail away, I don't know what I will do

Hoping, and Praying, that you change your mind

For I know that your Love, is one of a kind

But time is not on our side, and I Refuse to wait

I don't want to ever feel, like I am too late

Like a river to the sea, I will Stay by your Side

You are the only one that I want to Confide

So I will prepare myself, but I do not want us to ever again
Fight

But Please, I am going to need you to give me of A Lot
more than just One More Night!

©Joseph FbPoet Wilder2013

Cheating in the Next Room

Born N raised in ChitTown, where the Pimps up Hoes down was invented

So please don't think you have game, no matter how you try to spin it

Fb, Twitter, Tumblr, Instagram, etc. you are seen trying to make plans

Guess you are just too slow, to even understand

All of the love, I already know that you have been faking

Playing that cheating game, only BS is what you are making

Doing nothing more, but causing yourself unhappy days

But im not going to get caught up, in your tricky maze

Talking softly on the phone, and posting it all in these groups you think are ok

This isn't Burger King, you can't always have it your way

I thought we could still make it, so I went along

But you can't break my heart; it is now way too strong

So continue to give your rights to the internet, it can be your groom

I will just call it quits, and let you continue to Cheat Yourself in The Next Room!

©Joseph FbPoet Wilder2013

Never Be a Fool

I once believed that love was fair

Never wanted to be one to say, "That I don't Care"

In my heart I was sure that she was a friend

I never needed to say, " I swear to the end"

But it breaks my heart, when they all turn out the same

Don't want to feel, that love is just a game

Always knowing that it is both good, and bad in store

Just was not ready for my heart, to hit the floor

However I made the choice to take that risk

Never knowing you were the one that I had to frisk

No need to ask now, Love what have you done oh why

I cannot look back as we say goodbye

Trying to love someone, walking on a one way street

Never knowing, that you would be the one to mistreat

So just admit, a man is not what you want, you require a tool

N know that Never Again, Will I Ever Be A Fool!

©Joseph FbPoet Wilder2013

Fistful of Tears

You can Suck who you want to, and F()ck who you choose

I'm not the one out here playing to lose

From day one it has always been your choice

Even if it is another that makes you moist

We all are different, and have different desires

Some are upfront n honest, and some are liars

I will never judge you for what you like

That goes for if you are Straight, or choose to play with a Dyke

But like you make your choices, Know that I will make mine

Excuse me for My Desires, going deeper than just your behind

I'm a King, so does that mean I only want to fuck

Or is it fair to say that all Queens drop those drawls for a buck?

No it isn't, so no need for anyone to have Any fears

But I will Not be the one, with a Fist Full of Tears!!!

©Joseph FbPoet Wilder2014

Surrender

There is a story in my life

When you need AnyBody the Most, they are never around.

But they can all pop out the woodworks, when you hit the ground!

After all of the knowledge in life, that I have sowed,

My True Pain, can never ever be told.

The World is so messed up, and the game is so foul.

N that goes all the way back, to the First Mother N Child!

A Story of Pain, is in Each one of our lives.

But So Many are Hypocrites, and want to act surprised!

That is why you gotta keep it 100, and keep your circle tight.

Cus it is a Cold, Cold, Cold World, Not just at night!

See KARMA, is a MF, that act like a BITCH!

Don't have to be a Female, can be your Boy, down to a Snitch!

Times are so different now, and it is NoMore Loyalty.

Now it is Dollar Bills, that EveRyRyBody wanna See!

One of the main reasons, that it is hard for me to trust.

Always trying to figure out, What is True Love, or just Lust?

You Learn in Life, eveRyRybody that smile in your face, Aint your Friend.

When pain gets unbearable, Most wont be there till thE End!

Time, will let you know who your True Friends are.

Cus your True Friends, not about to let you slip underneath that bar!

We Learn though, that things don't always go the way we plan

N that the Ones who can cut you most, are closest friends to your Fam!

See it is not about racism, or even politics.

Like I said Before, we All know those hypocrites!

That always wants to front, and just smile in your face.

Then you find out, you done caught a case!

But we ALL need to FIRST step back, N Correct ALL of the harm that We do.

Cus Until then, I will NEVER be able to EVER,, SURRENDER TO ANY OF YOU!!!!!!!

Nice N Slow

I write about a lot but not much about me,

But is that something you are ready to see?

You can guess what is on my mind and that is a start.

But can you feel what is going on in my heart.

It's not about money or even sex,

N to be honest it's not really that complex.

But for Understanding you would really have to know JOE.

So please be gentle and take it Nice N Slow.

Hold Your Head Up

Why did he leave me here when the motorcycle gave me a spill.

But I know now that it is his will.

My whole life all I have wanted was for others to just Smile.

But for me would they walk that mile.

I learned through time we all experience our different pain.

But you can't let others drive you insane.

So its time to take that sec, and smile for all.

And hold your head high, because He won't let u fall.

Made in the USA
Middletown, DE
17 August 2016